INVESTING IN THE DREAM

BY

KENNY WOLFE

1

Ordering Information:
Quantity sales. Special discounts are available on quantity purchases by corporations, associations, and others.
Orders by U.S. trade bookstores and wholesalers. Please contact KENNY WOLFE via http://wolfe-investments.com

Edited and Marketed By
DreamStarters University
www.DreamStartersUniversity.com

"If you don't find a way to make money while you sleep, you will work until you die."

Warren Buffett

Table of Contents

Chapter 1

Too Good to be True?

Real estate has changed my life in more ways than you can imagine. To me, acquiring wealth was never about the houses and cars you can buy. It is, was, and always will be about **freedom**. Time is the one thing you can never get back. To be able to hop on a flight with my family and travel the world anytime we want is what I truly value. If you value the same, there is no better vehicle than multifamily real estate investing.

What would you do with an extra $500 every month? How about an extra $2,000? $5,000? $10,000? What kind of life would you be able to live if someone sent you a check for that amount regularly to your bank account or mailbox?

What worries would you be able to lay to rest? What new experiences in life would you be able to have? Where would you travel to if you could go anywhere and still be making money? Who would you be able to help? The majority of people don't ask themselves these questions, but they are the most important questions to figure out the answers to. You have to know where you want to go before you can begin.

What if you could get a check in your mailbox every single month, regardless of whether you went to work or not? You might be thinking, "That's impossible!" You might be thinking, "That sounds too good to be true." But this is neither impossible nor too good to be true. In fact, it's not just possible; it's necessary if you want to experience true financial freedom. And it's something my company has created for hundreds of people.

If you don't learn how to generate passive income as early as possible, you'll keep spending your time dependent on your 9-5 job. For most people, this is the reality they live with every single day. They are dependent on one revenue stream instead of having multiple revenue streams that mitigate the risk of solely relying on a job to provide for their family.

Don't get me wrong. There is nothing wrong with having a 9-5 job and working hard, but the truth is it's not solely a 9-5 job that creates serious wealth.

Focus, hard work, and drive are the keys to the equation when it comes to building long-term wealth and living the life of your dreams. The wealthiest people in the world know and make use of these factors to produce and keep growing money for themselves and their families.

The first part of the equation—which most people understand and will utilize for a good portion of their lives—is working a 9-5 job for money. There's nothing wrong with that, and that's how most folks have to start out. That's how I had to start out, and I learned a lot. But I knew that if I wanted to create wealth for our family, then that wasn't a long-term solution. So, that's not what this book is about.

The second part of the equation—which most people postpone having to learn until they're older—is making your money work for you. This is exactly what this book is about. As Warren Buffet, the most successful investor in the history of the world has said, "If you don't find a way to make money while you sleep, you will work until you die."

Work until you die? That sounds harsh, but that's the reality that many people live with. This doesn't have to be the case. There is a better way to live, and it involves creating multiple, passive revenue streams that keep money flowing into your bank account even when you're not at your job.

When you have multiple streams of passive income coming in, it's the best feeling in the world. It gives you more flexibility in life. You're not dependent on your job, your spouse's job, your pension, your social security checks or any one source of income to keep you afloat. If your boss disappoints you for the thousandth time, you can quit your job without worrying how you're going to pay your bills.

The best way that I've found to create multiple, passive income streams is by investing in real estate, particularly multifamily, commercial, lending, and development. Investing in real estate allows you to have your cake and eat it, too! It's the best investment to make if you want to generate passive income. Other types of investments can be more risky, less stable, and they don't produce as high of cash flow returns as real estate.

My wife and I learned this lesson the hard way when we bought an existing business right out of college. In our youthful exuberance, we fully trusted the financials we were given, went to six different banks to piece it together, and just knew we could eventually turn it into an absentee-owned business. We bought a small tanning salon, and it ended up doing okay if my wife worked in the business. My wife had to work there herself for it to make any money at all, and we quickly realized keeping it open was just not sustainable. It was not the life that either of us pictured for us long-term. As a result, we decided to take the loss, and we closed the business down.

When we closed down the tanning salon, I was still at my first job out of college, so we were fortunate to be able to weather the storm financially with relative ease. I worked as an accountant at an oil and gas firm in Dallas, Texas, and I made good money. My father was in oil and gas, and so was one of my grandfathers. I followed in their footsteps.

We experienced tremendous growth with an office of six and scaled to roughly 200 within a short time frame. I was promoted to an accounting manager for a new venture of that company. After just a few years, a mid-tier oil and gas company bought out the assets of the company I was working for. That same company kept our company around to continue leasing minerals on their behalf. They also wanted us to lease minerals in the Haynesville Shale, so I was promoted to a junior partner and CFO of the new oil and gas spinoff.

They sent myself, my wife (who was hired on to do administrative work), and a landman who was named the president (the person responsible for negotiating deals with landowners) and two managers to Shreveport, Louisiana to lease mineral rights. They entrusted us with $20 million and said, "Go figure it out." We quickly got to work.

In just three years, our initial small team grew from the original five of us to an eventual peak of 140 employees and independent contractors. Our company leased 32,000 acres and flipped them back to the mid-tier oil and gas company who was our sole client. When the mid-tier oil and gas company had money issues the first time, we were only two and a half years into our contract. My wife and I knew the company we were working for was the smaller dog in the contract, so our sole client would most likely be able to get out of the contract. Because of this, we started looking at different income opportunities.

After the tanning salon, we learned that we didn't want to buy another existing business that would require us to be too heavily involved in its day-to-day operations and management to make it profitable. We knew we had to look for a bigger opportunity, something that would allow us to have the cash available to hire other people to manage everyday operations for us.

We looked at passive oil and gas opportunities and invested in a few of those wells. We also looked at larger, more established businesses that had full-time employees already running them. But these didn't seem like the answer we were looking for. At the time, I didn't have the investors behind me needed to make that large of an acquisition. Also, with those types of investments, there's no easy way to get out the trapped equity unless you sell the whole business. This can be a lengthy and time-consuming process, and we decided it was something we didn't want to get ourselves into at that time.

After looking at all of the options, we realized that real estate was the clear winner. Banks love to loan money for real estate, so with the right team, it's easy to get a loan for the transaction. Also, there are many different ways to build equity in a property, and you can cash out trapped equity in the investment at certain points in the investment's holding period.

We did our research, and we joined a real estate group to learn the best ways to get started. We knew that we wanted to move from Shreveport, Louisiana back to Dallas, Texas. So we started looking at properties we could invest in that were located in the Dallas area. Initially, we considered buying 10 single family homes in the Dallas/Fort Worth area, but we quickly learned that multifamily real estate would allow us the ability to hire staff to run the day-to-day operations while I could focus on growing our portfolio of investments. Talk about living the dream!

We began by investing in real estate passively with two multifamily real estate investments to learn the ropes, and now the company I own is able to offer passive income opportunities to other investors. We're a full-blown, private equity real estate firm with a strong commitment to making our investors money.

This book is going to show you primarily how to become a deal sponsor like my company is for multifamily, commercial, hard money loans, and development real estate projects. A deal sponsor is the person or company who gets investors together (called syndication) to purchase a property to make money as a group. We look for either a value play, a yield play, or what I call a hybrid (discussed further in a later chapter of this book).

I had to learn how to do this through experience and through building the right team around me. There really is no substitute for experience in this industry because the real world is not static. Also, building the right team around you can cut down on the learning curve in a big way. Markets are always changing, and your experience as well as your team's experience are the only things that can put you in the best position to succeed in this business. This is why I have to implore you now, right at the beginning of this book, to commit yourself to learning through personal experience and start building your team.

This book is going to show you the steps I took to get to where I am now. Not enough books peel back the curtain on what it took someone to become successful. I'm going to show you how I got to the point where my small team has been involved in over $95 million worth of commercial real estate transactions all over the country. I'm going to shed some light on the possibilities that really are out there for you in the real estate industry to generate passive income for yourself and for others.

What you choose to do with this information is entirely up to you. Ultimately, you are the one who has to decide how much time and energy you want to invest in generating passive income through real estate. The opportunity is there for you to make a huge amount of money. Contrary to popular opinion, making money while you sleep is not too good to be true. **It's absolutely necessary if you want to live the life of your dreams.**

Invest Like a Wolfe

Hard work is only part of the equation when it comes to generating wealth. The other part of the equation is putting your wealth to work for you and generating passive income while you sleep. There are many paths to create wealth in America; I'm biased, but I believe real estate is the best vehicle to get you there. A lot of the other wealth generating options often require much more time commitment to working in the business and hoops to jump through when compared to avenues like real estate. In my opinion, real estate, specifically multifamily, commercial and development real estate projects are by far the most profitable form of passive income. It's one of the best investments you can make. In this book, I'm going to show how I've gotten to the point of being able to offer investment options as a deal sponsor to people who want to passively invest in real estate. Time is your most precious resource, so use it to your advantage.

"Most of my life I have done what I wanted to do. I have had fun on the job."

Walt Disney

Chapter 2

How I Got Started

My first taste of being an entrepreneur was when I was 10 years old. I went out to the country club near my home, and I sold used golf balls to the golfers out on the course. I collected all the used golf balls I could find out in the woods near the course, and then I sold them for a quarter a piece.

This venture only lasted about a day and a half. The country club ran me off when they found out what I was doing, but I got a taste for what happens when you look for an opportunity to make money for yourself instead of just taking a job and working for someone else.

At the age of 16, I started trading stocks. I didn't know what I was doing, but I got a taste of what playing the stock market is like. In the late 90s, prices were going way up.

This financial bubble quickly turned my meager $1,000 worth of investments into $10,000 worth of investments. I thought I was an *absolute genius* to have made this amount of money at 16 years old. After all, most kids my age were lucky if they made that much money working at a retail store or a fast food restaurant for an entire year.

I was on top of the world. I thought I was destined to become the next Warren Buffet by the time I graduated high school. But then it all came crashing down. I lost everything when the bubble burst right before my very eyes. I hadn't read *The Intelligent Investor* by Benjamin Graham or become the student of Warren Buffett I am today. Back then, I wasn't truly prepped with the knowledge it takes to trade stocks. I was extremely disappointed and was convinced that the stock market was a lot trickier than buying blindly and seeing the value rise.   I had sincerely believed I was smarter than everybody else, and I had bought into the "this time it's different" mentality that was going around in the 90s. The lesson I learned was that everybody else was just as dumb as me, and that whenever anyone says "this time it's different," get ready for value drop in whatever asset class they're talking about.

I learned that the stock market is a great place to put your money when it's going up. It's a great place to invest when you know the rules, the cycles and how to play to win. But I didn't know any of this stuff back then. I was just winging it, and what I was doing happened to work for a short period of time because of the momentum of the market. Experiencing the crash forced me to look for a better way to play the game of investing and to develop strategies to not only make money, but also to keep that money for the long-term.

Of course, I didn't like what happened to me back then. But in the long run it taught me the importance of knowing how to size up an investment by reading financials and understanding the actual business behind it. Understanding the long-term horizon of investments is so important.

Unfortunately, it's against human nature to think about long-term investing strategies. Humans tend to want instant gratification—that home run investment that doubles your money in less than a year. But instant gratification isn't the path to real wealth; investing truly is a marathon and not a sprint. The US tax code encourages longer-term investors as well, so if you're always looking for the quick buck, you're taxed at higher amounts.

In college, I read the book *Rich Dad, Poor Dad* by Robert Kiyosaki. This book really opened up my mind to the fact that there are a lot more options out there when it comes to building wealth for yourself and your family. You don't have to follow the path of working 40 years at the same company and putting as much money as you can into stocks, bonds and your 401k. That's what I was taught by my father, and it worked really well for him. That mentality is how about 95% of Americans believe saving for retirement should look.

There are other options available that most people don't even think about. I have always wanted to be an entrepreneur, but I wasn't sure which path I was going to take to get there. This book confirmed my suspicions that there were actually better ways to make money than working the traditional 9 to 5 J.O.B.

However, it took me several years to realize that real estate was my path to entrepreneurship. As mentioned in chapter one, I tried buying a small existing business, and I was involved in the oil and gas industry. Now I know that choosing to invest in the real estate industry was the best choice I could have ever made for my skill set. As a numbers guy who worked as an accountant and CFO for years, it plays to my inherent strengths in a lot of ways. Real estate, if done right, is all about numbers, not fixing toilets.

For those few that decide to break the mold on investing solely in the publicly traded markets and take the leap into real estate, I think most of them get into real estate and think the only way to make money is to buy a property that's in terrible shape for a low price, fix it up, and then flip it for a profit. Flipping properties has its place, but it's not the long-term wealth building investment that will put money in your pocket passively month after month. I've seen this mentality applied to the purchase and sale of both single family properties and multifamily apartment complexes.

I've seen people fix and flip 200 unit apartments, and this can mean a lot of money in the short-term. But this is leaving a lot of money on the table when it comes to the long-term earning potential of that same piece of property and the use of the tax shields I'm going to show you how to take advantage of relatively easily in this book.

If there's anything I've learned in all my experience, it's that there are enormous advantages to getting into the real estate investing game for the long-term. One of my favorite quotes is "Don't wait to buy real estate. Buy real estate and wait." Now, that doesn't mean to pay any price for a piece of property, but the idea is that those who hold real estate long-term will do better over the long run. Comparatively, there are very few reasons to invest in real estate for the short-term. This could be an effective tool to get you the capital needed to invest in a property that's a longer-term hold. It's not that there is no money to be had by putting your money into quick flip deals. You can earn money this way, but you miss out on the steady stream of cash flow that's actually possible if you hold onto the assets you purchase for a long time. The end goal should be that you make money whether you're at your job, in a hammock on the beach, at Disney World, or wherever.

One of the lessons I learned from my early experience in the stock market is there is much more risk involved in short-term investing strategies like fixing and flipping. If the housing market takes a dip at the wrong time, you might find yourself stuck with a high basis in a non cash-flowing property. It could be tough to satisfy your loan obligations, sell the investment to just break even, etc. When a market turns, a lot of folks who overpaid are all looking for the limited exit doors. This is why the old adage "slow and steady wins the race" is always true when it comes to investing. If you can't sleep easy each night due to your investments, then you're in the wrong investing game.

By making a few smart moves and learning how to identify a good property to invest in, you can build wealth not just for today, but for a lifetime. By delaying the desire for instant gratification, you can begin receiving quarterly checks for the rest of your life that can allow you to live the lifestyle you've always wanted to live.

Invest Like a Wolfe

My first ventures into entrepreneurship got shut down fairly quickly. The country club shut down my golf ball selling business within a couple of days, and the stock market taught me a valuable lesson about investing. Once I got involved in real estate investing, things started to click for me. It's the perfect match for my skills and expertise. By investing in real estate for the long-term, you too can build wealth for a lifetime. It is possible to get checks in the mail every month regardless of how much work you did. No matter what type of investing you do, always aim for long-term growth instead of short-term gain.

"The people who are crazy enough to think they can change the world are the ones who do."

Steve Jobs

Chapter 3

Go Big or Go Home

The oil and gas industry, which I worked in for many years, operates like a gigantic roller coaster ride—it's either feast or famine, and it can change in a hurry. Every industry experiences booms and busts, but in my opinion, nothing has wild swings like the oil and gas industry.

If you work in an industry as volatile as oil and gas, or maybe your pay is commission based, you have to do something to balance out all of the unknowns. You have to try to find a steadier source of revenue to shield you from the less certain paycheck revenue. This is one of the main reasons I was initially attracted to the real estate market. It's very stable compared to what I was used to, and it can be scalable, so I could further mitigate any ups or downs in the industry with multiple investments, creating different revenue streams.

There are a lot of people who experience major fluctuations in their income from month to month and year to year. I have friends who are sales reps and in other types of jobs that have fluctuating paychecks from month to month.

Now what if those folks are the sole breadwinners in their households? They typically don't get paid a huge yearly salary. Most of their income—and thus their family's income—comes from sales commissions. This makes it very difficult for them to know what the family budget should be each month. Passive income from real estate investments is the perfect antidote to this problem. Another source of income can smooth over these swings in paychecks. How freeing would it be to worry less about your main source of income?

The goal when investing is to have multiple passive revenue streams, and we focus on real estate as the way to create those streams. Why wait to worry about learning to create passive income when you're near retirement? Get started early, so you can build and enjoy that cash flow at a younger age. It can take time to build a strong portfolio, so patience is key. I see a lot of investors forcing it these days, and eventually when the tide of the market turns, it will take a lot of these "investors" out to sea. So be patient; it doesn't happen overnight. If you rush things, or invest because you HAVE to have retirement income, you're more prone to make a mistake, and that can be very costly.

In my opinion, one passive revenue stream is good, but two is even better. Four is amazing because even if one or two streams of revenue drop off temporarily for some reason, there's still money coming in. If something goes wrong at one property, your checkbook might take a hit, but you should be able to weather the storm.

Now, investing in multifamily, commercial, or development properties can take a little bit of a bigger checkbook to get into, because you're dealing with a lot more zeros when you invest in larger properties. This does weed out a lot of the competition, but it doesn't mean you can't get into these types of real estate investments; it's just much more difficult.

I've seen people invest in multifamily properties with as little as $15,000, but they are the exception to the rule. A more serious deal typically requires an initial investment of at least $50,000 or more to get it acquired correctly.

When I decided I wanted to get started in real estate investing, I did a lot of reading on the subject. I built quite the library! There are so many books out there with great information. Of course, you have to know how to take that book knowledge and see how it applies to the real world and the markets you want to make your real estate investments in. So I joined two local real estate groups. These groups helped me to find the first two passive deals in real estate I ever did, and they coached me through my first syndication.

The first property I found to passively invest was a value play in Arlington, Texas. A value play is a property that is selling for less than its replacement cost (most of the time WAY less than replacement cost) because of its condition, or a variety of other factors. These types of plays tend to be low on cash flow at first (sometimes negative cash flow), but have a great chance for outsized appreciation. Value is created for investors by improving the property either with physical improvements to the properties, through improved management of the operations, or both. Once the property is stabilized, you can either sell the property and take the profits, or re-finance and get cash out of the property in a tax-deferred manner. *(Please note, I'm not a CPA or lawyer, so please consult before engaging in any deal on your own.)*

If you sell the property, you'll get all of the profit out, minus the transactional fees to sell the property and capital gains tax to pay. If you keep the property and re-finance it, then typically you do not pay taxes on the cash you get back at the closing of the re-finance. Also, you keep a cash flowing asset, and your residents are paying down the higher loan you just took out.

This first value play I passively invested in was your typical fixer upper that was going to need to be rehabbed before it was going to start making money. It was the worst property on its block, and there were cars on literal blocks in the parking lot. We were told that the local pizza delivery guy wouldn't even go into the property to deliver pizzas—it was that bad. We did buy that property for $13k a door out of a foreclosure, and the bank that owned the property even lent us money to buy it and fix it up. They wanted it off of their non-performing balance sheet.

The second property I found to passively invest in was a yield play. Meaning, it was pretty much fixed up and generating cash flow as soon as it was purchased. I passively invested in both of these properties at about the same time so I could learn the ropes of how syndicated deals come together, and how each polar opposite deal type performed. A syndication is when a group of investors pool their money together to buy an investment. They then share the cash flow and other profits that are generated from the investment. (This is how we structure our investments at Wolfe Investments for our investors.)

Both of the properties I invested in passively turned out to be great investments, so I decided to gear up to put together my first syndicated deal in which I would play the role of deal sponsor. I orchestrated my first syndicated deal just two years after making those first two passive investments.

The ability to acquire properties and generate a return for investors requires a significant amount of education, knowhow and experience. I learned as much as I could from books, and even more by getting involved in passive deals on my own. There's no substitute for real world experience when it comes to real estate. Sometimes deals look great on paper, but they throw you curveballs while operating them, markets change during the hold period, or you discover ways to further improve the property after you have purchased the property.

Here's an example everyone can relate to, regardless of your experience in real estate. Have you ever looked at a property for sale online that looked incredible? In the pictures, it might look like the property is worth thousands more than the asking price. But when you see the property in person, and you start to dig into the details of the property, suddenly the whole picture changes. It's amazing what brokers can make a dumpy property look like with tightly shot photos, and I've even seen some Photoshop going on.

You have to be very careful when purchasing any type of real estate, and there are many more things to analyze before you pull the trigger on a larger transaction—especially if you have other people's money involved. If you make a mistake, and purchase a property that's not profitable, then it can seriously tarnish your reputation as a syndicator who is worth investing with. All syndicators will eventually make at least a small mistake, and it's there that you see who the good syndicators are—by how they right the ship. A good syndicator is willing to do whatever it takes to right it.

To give you an example, one of the things I learned from experience is that if you buy a property that has less than 60 units, you have to get creative to be able to afford full-time, onsite management and maintenance staff. With less revenue coming in due to having fewer renters in the building, you have less money available to hire people to run things for you. If you're not careful, you might find yourself changing toilets and giving apartment tours.

Once you start having to work in your business at your properties, you're no longer able to focus on growing your portfolio of properties which will slow down your ability to create more passive income. You're setting yourself up for the same headache you were trying to avoid. You don't need another full-time job. You don't need to work for more dollars. You need your dollars to work for you.

The general rule of thumb is for every 100 multifamily units you can afford a full-time manager and a full-time maintenance person. If there are fewer than 100 units in a property you're considering, then you have to know how you are going to address the less staff you can afford.

The first property I ever bought was 76 units in Wylie, Texas. Since this first syndication was 76 units, it meant that we had to work out how to properly staff the property. For this particular property we operate with a full-time manager and a part-time maintenance person. Each property is different, but as this was a newer property, and we put a lot of capital expense into the property up front, we're able to operate this way. There are not a lot of people who are willing to work part-time maintenance, so that's where it's important to find the right management company that can make it work. By being able to afford a professional management company, you can cover the nuances of each property. If a management company is big enough, then they may have an answer by already managing a property down the street, or they may have a floating maintenance person to fit your property's needs.

My desire is to never be bogged down by the day-to-day maintenance or operations of the properties I own. If I had to take care of all of the daily activities at my properties, then I wouldn't be able to focus on buying more properties and building a strong portfolio for investors. My passion and true value creation comes from creating good investments for our investors.

The big lesson here is to go big or go home. If I were to have started out by buying smaller 10 to 20-unit, multifamily properties, then there is no possible way I could have afforded to hire other people to run them for me. I would have been stuck being the person who would have to evict people, collect rents and change toilets. There is no way I would have grown our portfolio of multifamily, commercial, hard money loans, and development projects if I was bogged down in day-to-day operations.

Because I have only ever invested in large apartment complexes, these duties have never fallen to me. I don't know even know the steps on how to evict anybody, even though this happens monthly across our multifamily portfolio. There are people who break their lease agreement every month, but our great onsite staff take care of that aspect of the business. The wonderful managers we've put in place at the properties not only take care of the evictions, but leasing units, making sure the property looks great, making sure units are to our specifications for new residents, etc., and that's exactly how I want it to be.

I have no idea how to change a toilet, and I don't want to know. I also have a hard and fast rule that I don't touch the keys at the property, nor do I have keys to any of the properties' offices. I'm focused on making sure our current assets are performing, as well as growing our portfolio. Again, if I were focused on the granular, day-to-day operations, it would slow down the investment options Wolfe Investments can offer investors.

A neighbor of mine recently discovered the importance of going big or going home. He owns 30 units near where we own our 76 unit multifamily property. A few years ago there was a huge hailstorm that came through our area. We all got pelted with softball size, Biblical hail. It did massive damage to all of the properties in our area. There were 96 spots where the hail went through the roof, and I mean through past the decking. It was amazing no one was injured in that storm.

Since we were a larger property, we had more buying power and more cash so we were able to act fast and get our apartments fixed up quickly. The very next day after the storm, we cleaned up all the glass we could. We bought all the windows we could get our hands on. I knew there was going to be a shortage of them because the hailstorm was so widespread and the damage so great. Everyone in that part of town had lots of repair work and insurance claims to file. That meant a big demand for windows, roofing, siding, etc.

Our team went to work, bought wood to board up the windows that were broken, and we were able to allow almost all of our tenants to remain on the property. Our focus was to provide watertight units and windows as fast as possible for our residents to make sure that we were once again the best property for the best price in the area. With all of the other properties being slower to respond, we were able to help almost everyone stay in their homes with as little disruption to their lives as possible. This also had a beneficial effect on our occupancy and, therefore, our revenues remained relatively constant.

My neighbor didn't act as fast we did; in fact, most of our competition didn't act near as fast as we did. His property was smaller, and he was forced to go down to 50% occupancy while repairs were being made to the property because of the extent of the damage.

We bought what we needed to fix our apartment immediately, and then we got reimbursed by our insurance company. Our occupancy didn't take a hit. Our cash flow was a little wonky in the short-term, but our residents were happy, and we ended up having much smoother revenue than our neighbors. Our neighbor had a messy two years trying to square everything away with his one property. He didn't have as much staff available to clean up the problem as we did. He had to be a lot more hands-on than I did. This is not my idea of passive income.

You can see, there are a whole host of reasons it pays to go big. It's easier to buy a bigger property in the long run than it is to buy a smaller property. Too often people sell themselves short on how big they can go. But to put it in the simplest terms possible: the more legs you have under you, the easier it is to keep your balance. You don't want one problem to be able to completely knock you over.

Invest Like a Wolfe

When it comes to investing in real estate, it's either go big or go home. If the properties you buy are too small, you will have a difficult time generating truly passive income from them. The rule I follow is that I won't invest in a property unless it has at least 100 units. This means the property has the potential to generate enough revenue for me to be able to pay for full-time maintenance and management. Similarly, it's best to have ownership of multiple properties so you have deep pockets that can help you maintain if something goes wrong at one of your properties. The more legs you have under you, the easier it is to keep your balance when you get knocked around.

"Someone's sitting in the shade today because someone planted a tree a long time ago."

Warren Buffett

Chapter 4

Weigh Your Options Carefully

When people first get started investing in real estate, they often focus on one city. While that might work when your local market is depressed, it doesn't work so well in a hot market. For example, I have a colleague who started out about the same time as I did, and he only focused on the Dallas-Fort Worth area. He's grown a lot more slowly than I have because he wasn't willing to invest in other markets like I have. Besides the properties I have in Texas, myself and my investor group own properties in Oklahoma, Louisiana and Ohio. We're also looking to add other states to this list as well.

If you only focus on investing in one city, it slows down your deal flow. And with such a hot market these days, you have to look at 100 deals to find one good one. I was getting frustrated with our local real estate prices in DFW, so I took a drive to Oklahoma City to check it out. On the way home I had one of those "aha" moments: if I was willing to drive 2.5 hours one way, then why not fly? That really opened up the playing field and eventually took us beyond Texas in our real estate holdings. We still buy in Texas because it's our back yard, but now we look in multiple states, which really increases our deal flow.

Another down side of only focusing on one area is you can't take advantage of the varying costs of real estate across the country. For example, if I sell a property in a hot market, then it will be harder to find a property to do a 1031 exchange into if I'm only focused on buying property in that same hot market.

When we've performed our business model for a property, we've trapped equity in the property. One way to get that out in a tax-deferred manner is to do a 1031 exchange. A 1031 exchange allows us to defer paying taxes on the money our investor group has made from selling the property as long as we invest the money into another property. *(Please consult your CPA for 1031 exchange details.)*

So, if we do a 1031 exchange, and we sell in a hot market and buy in a softer market where prices are not inflated, we have the ability to find another great investment property. A 1031 exchange allows us to delay the capital gains on the property, which gives us the opportunity to take what we would have paid in taxes, and put it to work in our next real estate transaction. It's a way to compound our real estate returns.

If you buy in a market where there is less competition, then you're more likely to find better properties. You want to make sure that the city meets certain criteria before you buy there, but I've seen it many times when I've bought in a new city for our investors and then the word gets out about that location as a great place to invest. If there are a lot of fishermen in one section of the lake, then you need to find a new place to fish. When you pigeonhole yourself to just one city, you're doing your investors a disservice. That also carries over to different real estate investments as well. That's why we began to offer investments in hard money loans and commercial properties alongside our multifamily offerings.

One of the first questions I often get from new investors is, "What cities and locations should I invest in?" The number one thing I look at is whether or not a state is landlord friendly. The top five landlord friendly states are currently Texas, Indiana, Colorado, Arizona and Florida. Other states can be just as close to being landlord friendly, but any state where the tenants can drag out eviction for months is no good. The investor has to pay their mortgage during that time they're not getting rent.

The number two thing I look at are the cities within the state and how economically diverse they are. If a city has a limited amount of employers, or has a higher exposure to one industry, then there's more risk for your property. For example, if you look at Midland-Odessa, you can see that it is not an economically diverse area. The economy there is driven by oil and gas. So if you're buying into the real estate market there, what you're really buying into is oil and gas. If oil drops from 100 to 50 dollars a barrel, then the apartments there are not going to do well. People are going to move out, and they're going to move away from that area. It may be a good move to buy there when oil drops, but the lending in these parts of the country can make it difficult to get decent terms.

Military towns present the same issue. Military folks are great residents, some of the best you can have. Our experience has been that the units we've had military residents in we get back with very minimal wear and tear. The problem they present to landlords is deployment. If there are a high percentage of military residents living in your apartments, and there is a deployment, they're able to break their lease. While I respect and applaud all of those that serve in the military, the unknown risk at a property in those towns can be really tough on the investment. Empty units do not pay the mortgage, but if you're a landlord in a military town, it's something you're going to have to deal with regularly.

I have a colleague that owns a property down in Killeen, Texas. There's a military base located there called Fort Hood, and it employs a large percentage of the residents who live there. My colleague has told me that he wishes he had never bought a rental property there because he is often at 95 percent capacity for four to six months, but when there's a deployment, he crashes down to 80 percent capacity. This totally kills his cash flow. He has to pour in a lot of money at once to get the units ready for new tenants each time and there's the extra cost of trying to fill the property again.

You don't want to put your hard earned investment dollars into the hands of any one industry. The goal to investing is to get the highest return for the least amount of risk. You always have to look at the downside and mitigate those risks.

The third item I look at is the historical economic growth, population trends, and unemployment. These things are very important for a real estate investor to know. If the population is stagnant or declining, then it is going to be hard to fill your multifamily property or have your commercial tenants earn enough revenue to pay rent. Historical unemployment is important because if there are lost jobs, then how will your residents pay rent? I look for growing cities, and the sooner I get there before other investors, the better the investment for our investors.

The fourth thing I look at when considering where to purchase a property is more granular. I look at the demographics of the sub-market within the city. I look at median income, crime rates, etc. Median income and crime rates are the most important in my book. Another quick rule of thumb I use is that if a property is being sold on par with the median income in its neighborhood, then I'm interested in purchasing it. If it's being sold for what could be considered double the median income, then I don't go for it. That listing goes straight to the trash icon! That means the market is way out of whack; either paychecks will have to grow considerably, or rents will have to go down. Something has to give. At the time of this writing, we're seeing a lot of investors willing to pay double the median income on a per door price for a multifamily property.

For example, there's a multifamily property down in the Grand Prairie, Texas area here currently for sale. It's actually the first apartment my wife and I ever lived in when we moved up to DFW out of college. It wasn't very nice, and I was amazed every morning that my motorcycle was still there. But since we lived there, I was curious to see what the seller wanted for the property. The median income in that area is about $36,000. The asking price for the property is about $70,000 per unit. This means that residents' rent has to start creeping up past 33% of their take home pay, or there has to be more residents per unit to share the higher rent. Residents can't do that in the long run. It's not sustainable.

Paychecks haven't kept up, yet we're at 5-6 percent annual rent growth across the majority of the nation for the last six years. Many people in the markets are just now worried about inflation, but we've had housing inflation in huge leaps and bounds for years. Housing plays a huge role in calculating inflation as it typically takes up a large portion of a person's paycheck.

Take, for example, someone who works as a Starbucks barista. You can't bill them $50 more a month every year for rent because they just aren't getting paid more. It just doesn't work out long-term. This is why I look for median income compared to the price per unit we would have to ask for to remain profitable. Remember, for me, it's all about long-term cash flow potential. If an investment isn't going to hold up over time, I'm not interested. I'm not interested in solely appreciation plays hoping someone less intelligent than me comes along and overpays. There's a difference between speculators and investors.

Sometimes, even when everything looks good on paper, something will come up with a property that makes it not worth buying. There was a beautiful property in Oklahoma City I was very interested in. A newly revamped medical center across the street, Starbucks was on the opposite corner, and other retail within close walking distance. I was told by the seller that in the 1980s there had been a dry cleaner across the street that used a very nasty, hazardous chemical that had seeped into the ground, but all that cleanup effort was behind the property.

It turned out that the building had already been cleared by the Oklahoma Environmental Commission, but it had not been cleared by the EPA. The EPA wanted to drill down into the ground, steam it and see what chemicals came out. If any of the hazardous chemical came out, then the owner would have had to put a special fan in each unit to make sure the property was safe to live in. I don't ever want our properties to be potentially hazardous to our residents. So, I passed on the deal. Our aim is make our residents happy and offer the best product at the best price. You can't do that when a property has potential lingering issues.

In my mind, even if I did everything I could to protect the residents of the property, I didn't want to have to worry about that nasty chemical in the long run. Even though the property looked great and the numbers checked out, it was too much liability for me and our investors to assume. In the end, it just wasn't worth the risk. Canceling the contract was the right thing to do to protect myself and the other investors.

As you can see, there are a lot of factors to consider when you're looking at buying a property, so doing your due diligence in every way you can is important. When you're playing the long game, you must weigh your options carefully.

Invest Like a Wolfe

Investing in real estate in diversified markets allows you to sell in a hot market and buy in soft market. When you do this and take advantage of a 1031 exchange, you are able to potentially compound your gains from the prior property. To judge whether or not a certain market is worth entering, the first thing you need to look at is whether the state you're looking in is landlord friendly. Second, it needs to have diverse economic drivers. Third, the city has to have good historical growth in population, low unemployment, and economic growth. Fourth, the property itself needs to be available at a price roughly on par with median income for its area. Don't forget to consider any other extraneous variables that might make a property less valuable than it appears. Always weigh your options carefully.

"When you're playing the long game, you must weigh your options carefully."

Kenny Wolfe

Chapter 5

The Safest Path

I've always wanted to be an entrepreneur. I like having control over my own destiny. It's always been a big deal for me to be able to be the captain of my own ship.

But giving up a steady monthly paycheck from an employer can be a very scary thing to do. Especially if, like me, you have a family who is counting on you to put food on the table every month. When you decide it's time to bet on yourself, you have to think about how you're going to make it work when you're just getting started.

When you first start any type of business, it can take time to build up your clientele and cash flow. With some startups you never know where your next dollar is going to come from. There are two approaches you can take to solving this problem and making sure you don't get in a cash crunch chasing your dreams.

The first approach is to save up as much money from your 9-5 job as you possibly can. How much you need to save before you take that leap of faith is entirely dependent on your household expenses and your lifestyle. Also, if you believe you can go back to your job or a similar job easily, then you might decide to save less money before you quit your job than someone who believes they will have a difficult time finding comparable employment if things don't pan out with their business. Always have a good plan B!

The second approach you can take—and the one I took—is you can get a part-time job so you are only responsible for bringing in a portion of your typical income while your business is getting started. This is a good option because it allows you to slowly and properly build your business without needing to focus on short-term cash flow needs every month.

If you're desperate for cash, you become willing to compromise your values and investment goals just to make ends meet. The added stress from dependents could force you to make riskier investment decisions as you may feel pressured for cash flow now and not take into account the long-term investment ramifications. It is a much better idea to build a proper foundation for the long-term success of your business than to have to focus on short-term profits merely for your own survival.

When I wanted to get into real estate, I took a part-time accounting job so I could work on my business during the extra hours I had available each week. I knew I needed to have a paycheck coming in while I was getting established. In my opinion, this is the best way to get started—even if you have a lot of money saved, this offsets the risks associated with entrepreneurship considerably. A part-time job keeps money flowing in while you're still figuring things out.

If you want to start a business that deals in larger real estate investments (which I imagine is the case if you're reading this book), you have to give yourself a lot of time to find your first property. In hot markets like they are now, you have to look at 100 different properties just to find one that's worth buying. There are challenges in every part of the market cycle, which could cause some delay in finding the right deal. Right now the issue is finding truly solid investments, but seven years ago the issue was finding the investors and financing. If it were easy, everyone would do it!

Finding the right property can mean passive cash flow for the rest of your life. So buying an investment property requires a lot of careful analysis before you pull the trigger. For these larger transactions, you're in charge of other people's money, and the transactions have more zeros than say a single family investment. It's literally a decision that's going to impact your life and your investors' lives forever.

If you want to be in investment real estate, and you quit your job today, it's going to be tough. You have to look through a lot of deals before you find a good one. This takes time, and you never know when money is going to come in. Keeping a job on the side is the best way to stay afloat while you learn the ropes of this business. The market in your area and many other factors will influence how fast the process goes for you.

You can't afford to get yourself involved in a bad deal on your first one. If you do, then you're done. No one is going to invest with you ever again if your first deal melts down. So when you're doing your first deal, you want to focus on acquiring a property that has cash flow already. Don't purchase a high-risk, high-reward property.

I suggest finding a property that will allow you to send out investor distributions quickly, as there is no better marketing material out there! If you go out and buy a fixer upper on your first deal, then you're going to be delayed on sending out investor distributions, and you will be jumping into a very large project your first time in the business. I've seen it work once for a colleague, but only the once. You have to play this game the smart way, or you won't be playing for very long.

When I took a part-time accounting gig, I did it so I could set myself up for long-term success. I came to an agreement with my employer that I would be able to go out at lunch or leave work early to look at deals if I needed to. I looked at a lot of deals before finally pulling the trigger.

You want to have your first property humming along nicely before you buy a second one. Otherwise, I've seen syndicators end up way out over their skis. I've been a part of three real estate investment rescues where I wasn't the initial asset manager or syndicator. In two of these situations, I started out as a passive investor, and I was voted in by the other investors to turn things around.

The third rescue I was voted in to save I wasn't even an initial investor. It was a huge fixer-upper in which the investor group paid too much money upfront, overspent on the rehab, and was taking too long to lease up. I knew some of the folks who had invested in the property, and they asked me to turn it around. I always hate to see investors lose money, so I took on the project. It was also in the best interest of the neighborhood as a whole to make sure it didn't collapse, as it was the eyesore on the block.

The deal sponsor who put together these deals I had to save is no longer able to raise money for deals. Would you, as a passive investor, invest with someone again who nearly had a property taken back by the lender? No way! In fact, his business is pretty much done unless he somehow finds investors who aren't aware of how his other deals turned out.

Now that I own properties myself and have looked at a countless number of them, I know what amenities work and don't work. I know what it takes to make a property profitable. Now I'm able to see what the residents want and offer it to them. When other owners are filling in pools, not putting in dog parks, and making other shortsighted property decisions, they're missing out on attracting the best residents.

But this knowledge didn't come to me overnight. I had to invest in learning it through books, seminars, workshops and mentors. I also had to spend time in the real world of real estate acquainting myself with the everyday ins and outs of the business. You learn the best by being knee deep in the investment.

If you want to succeed and become a trusted deal sponsor like I have, take your time learning all you can about this business. This book is a fantastic resource for you, but there's no denying you will need to read many more before you are an expert. Also, don't be shy about secret shopping properties to get a feel for the rents, quality of the unit interiors and property amenities.

It may be tempting to want to rush into becoming a full-time real estate entrepreneur, but my advice is to slow down, and make sure to do it right. The safest path into entrepreneurship is to find a way to work on your business while you still have income coming in through a part-time job or another source. Remember, running your own business, no matter what type, is not a sprint. It's a marathon.

Invest Like a Wolfe

The best way to start a business is to have a part-time job, and work on your business in the extra hours you have available. This allows you to not worry so much about the money your business is bringing in to start. Especially in the business of large real estate acquisitions, it is important to build a strong foundation. The first deal you do is the most important. It must succeed, so you can't rush it. Running a successful business is not a sprint. It's a marathon.

"The safest path into entrepreneurship is to find a way to work on your business while you still have income coming in through a part-time job or another source."

Kenny Wolfe

Chapter 6

Your First Multi-Family Property

There are a few big things you always want to look at when you're considering purchasing a multifamily rental property, or really any income producing property at that. It's best to have knowledge of proper building construction, or work with someone who knows how to analyze the strengths and weaknesses of a property before you commit to purchasing it. Due diligence is a must!

The first thing you need to look at is the foundation of the building itself. In North Texas, it's not if you have foundation issues, but when you'll have foundation issues as we have lots of clay soil here. In other parts of the country there is a lot less ground movement, so if there are foundation issues there, then the issues tend to be more serious.

Figure out how the area's soil relates to any movement in the ground. If there are problems with the foundation, you have to crunch the numbers and see if your budget allows you to fix it. If it doesn't, then either the seller needs to come down in price, or you move on. The age of the roof is also a big deal because eventually that will have to be repaired or replaced, especially if you plan on holding the property long term. It's hard to tell from the ground if a roof has issues, so I always have a roofer come out and inspect it. You don't want any surprises.

Another thing I always take a look at is the heating and air conditioning system. Is it a chiller system, or individual HVAC? I prefer individual HVAC, but even then you need to see how old the units are and make replacement plans accordingly. Having your heating and air conditioning system fail is unacceptable for residents, so we aim to have those systems inspected thoroughly upfront and before every heating and cooling season. If one causes an issue, then that's a priority work order that gets done.

I also look at exterior items like the type of siding material, exterior paint, the parking lot and landscaping. Do we need to spruce up the paint to give it curb appeal? Does the parking lot have major potholes? What does the property sign look like, and how can we improve it?

I try to decide if there are any amenities we could add or improve like a pergola or BBQ grill area for the residents, pool area improvements, or covered parking options. If we can add a dog park, then I try to squeeze one of those in for sure. These types of add-ons are a good way to attract better quality residents who are looking for a better product than your immediate competition.

Interior wise, I look at the flooring, the kitchens, the appliance packages, and the bathroom features that are currently offered at the property. To get a feel for what the renters' expectations are for a certain area, I take a look at neighboring properties. I'll do "secret shopping" and look at other apartments' exteriors, interiors, amenities and the rent they demand compared to the property I'm planning to purchase. It's also nice to see what kind of customer service your potential competition offers; that alone can be a reason for a resident to move away from a property.

Your first multifamily property will be the most difficult for you to purchase. It's a lot bigger transaction, the steps are different, and the buyers and sellers tend to be more sophisticated. It also will take a while for brokers and buyers to take you seriously as a first timer as these acquisitions take a certain level of sophistication and bigger amounts of cash. The loans are larger and take a higher net worth statement. And due to their size, typically they require raising funds from outside investors. So you'll have to convince a seller that you can perform as a buyer.

Often there is an interview process you have to go through in order to be determined eligible to buy the property. The buyer and broker are typically on the phone call and ask questions to see how prepared you are, and to make sure you know what you're doing. No one wants to waste time with someone who can't close a transaction. Also, if you are working with other investors like I do, you have to follow SEC guidelines, and make sure you're compliant. The SEC comes into play because you're selling shares of the newly formed entity that will purchase the property.

Once you have made your very first purchase of a multifamily property, then it gets easier from there. When you're established as someone who knows what they're doing with a multifamily property and can close a transaction, then that brings down some of the barriers you face when you're just getting started. As with any business, once you've built up momentum and a solid reputation, things begin to snowball from there.

It's also a good idea to look in multiple markets to increase your deal flow and tap into other markets that have less buying competition. Go fish where other people aren't fishing. For example, Dallas-Fort Worth is on the national scene at the moment. Those of us in the real estate market here have to compete against both local and foreign investors from all over the world who want to buy in this market. All of these outside folks are coming in and bidding up the prices in this area because they've been told the story of how our population is growing and how large corporations are moving in.

All that is true, but in my opinion, that story has been oversold for a while here. So I started looking elsewhere like Oklahoma City, Colorado Springs, Cincinnati etc. None of the outside, foreign investors are looking there. Some of these places aren't attractive outsiders, but they're really great markets. If you've never been to an Oklahoma City Thunder game and hung out in Bricktown, then you're missing out! They have steady growth, diverse economic drivers, are landlord friendly, etc.

Of course, if you are doing business in multiple markets, you might still face some challenges when entering a new market. Often times we'll have to buy a smaller property than we would have liked to show to the local owners and brokers that we can close out of state transactions. Now that we've done that a few times it's not as difficult to persuade them. When you're the "new guy," you have to prove yourself.

When I first bought an out of state property in Colorado Springs, I had to convince the seller and broker that we could close the deal. I actually had our lender meet me at the property tour, so the selling broker could see how serious I was. It pays to have a great team! I had a similar experience, although not to the same degree as the first out of state acquisition when we went into Ohio. I could tell that everyone thought, "What is this Texan doing wanting to buy in Columbus, Ohio?" They weren't sure what to think about me.

They didn't know why I was there, or why I was interested in properties in Ohio.

But I bought a smaller property in the Columbus market first, just to get established there. Then we bought an 120 unit, late 70s property that is just beautiful. I wanted them all to see that I was legitimate. After that, I bought the larger property, and no one had an issue with it. As with most things in life, getting started is always the hardest part.

When I first started venturing out into different markets that were not right in our backyard, I wasn't sure how it was going to go. It meant moving out of my comfort zone a little bit, and to a big degree there was convincing of our investors that needed done. The investors had seen my track record here locally, but I had to convince them that by going out of state we could widen our investment possibilities.

Since we have onsite staff that handles the day-to-day operations, it really opens up the playing field on locations we can buy. If you had to perform a portion of the day-to-day tasks, you would be stuck within a pretty small radius of your first acquisition. We make sure to hire quality onsite staff as this improves the quality of living for our residents, and it requires us less onsite visits. We visit our properties multiple times a year, sometimes announced and other times unannounced to keep everyone on their toes. Because our job is to manage the asset and team handling the day-to-day management, we can do this comfortably from our office in Plano, Texas.

Whether our properties are local or out of state, I only visit them four to five times a year. That number increases when we have a new acquisition, or if we have rehab projects going on, or if the numbers dip on a property. When the numbers dip, we take a trip. But if I show up at a property for no reason, I'm wasting the management's time. She can't collect rent, lease units, handle evictions, etc. with me there. The staff are focused on me, when I'd rather them focus on the operations of the property.

It is obviously necessary to visit your properties and tend to your large investments, but if you're able to hire a full-time staff, it decreases the need for your onsite property check ups. My goal is to keep my visits to a maximum of 30 minutes if at all possible. Sometimes there are items that may make the visit longer (rehab projects, etc.), but even then the visits are short and sweet.

I receive daily or weekly reports about our properties, so I can monitor them that way. And we're able to quickly make phone calls if need be, so we're in constant contact with the management company tending to our asset. Making sure things are running smoothly doesn't require a lot of hands on work if you set things up correctly, which was my main goal for getting into this line of business in the first place.

I wanted my focus to be on growing our portfolio and not fixing toilets. By starting out buying larger properties, we were able to afford a third-party management company. This meant I could safely monitor them from a distance. It allows a buyer to own properties anywhere and be confident they are in good hands without having to visit them daily.

Now, the challenge for someone just getting started is finding the right third-party management company to run things for you. There are a lot of bad to mediocre ones out there. I've had success with the management companies that we've used on our properties, but the majority of them have had some issues that I have had to deal with as there weren't very many decent alternative management companies out there.

This is why recently I've partnered with an existing property management company where the owner and I can create the best management company out there. With his, and his teams' property management experience, and my perspective as an investor, we can build a much better product for our owners. I'm very excited about this new venture. Not just for the better results we'll get by bringing our management company in-house, but for the other investors we can help maximize their properties' potentials. We're going to create a lot of value in the market place.

The process for finding a management company is going to vary quite a bit from person to person because it's all about networking and finding people who you believe will do the job you want them to do. When I was first starting out, I asked local selling brokers, mortgage brokers, and other property owners who they liked as a management company.

Another options is to look online and find what management companies are located in the area you want to buy in. I typically buy B and C class assets, so I'm looking for management companies that have an expertise with these types of assets. B class assets are typically between 15 and 30 years old, and they are in less sought after neighborhoods than A class assets. C class assets are typically more than 30 years old, and they are generally found in low income neighborhoods. These rules of thumb can be broken if a property's location is in a premier spot, the property is well taken care of, and the property gets premium rent. Rent per square foot comparisons are sometimes a better way to tell a property's asset class than its age.

If you're buying B and C class assets like I do, then don't look for a management company that manages A class assets. B and C class assets require a different type of management company, and companies that do A class asset management are usually not a good fit for B and C assets. Don't try and fit a square peg into a round hole.

When you find a management company that looks like they might be a good fit for your property, go check out the properties they currently manage. I typically don't tell them I'm going to visit some of their current properties when we first start talking. If you show up unannounced, then the grounds, and level of service will be as they normally are from day-to-day. They won't have tried to make everything look especially good for your arrival.

For single family rentals, paying a management company to run things for you usually costs you about 8 to 10 percent of the income from the property. This is a pretty significant amount and eats heavily into your profits.

The good thing about multifamily is—since the income is naturally much higher—the management company typically requires 3.5 to 4 percent for managing your property. If the property is smaller, then this percentage goes up as high as 6 percent from what I've seen. On top of that percentage, you will also be responsible to pay the onsite payroll even though those employees are typically employees of the management company. But this cost is well worth it when you consider that all the day-to-day stuff is handled exclusively by the management company.

If you choose your property and management company carefully, you can truly generate passive income with ease. It requires a lot of careful analysis to be able to do this properly for the first time, but if you do it right, the reward is immense.

Invest Like a Wolfe

There are many factors you need to take into consideration when purchasing your first multifamily property. Being familiar with the requirements of proper building construction is important. If you're not knowledgeable in this area, find someone to work with who is. Buying your first property is going to be the biggest challenge. Until you have built up a reputation for yourself, you will have to work hard to gain the trust of the people in this industry. Once you've purchased your first property, the next one will come easier. Finding the right management company to run things for you is absolutely critical if you want to generate truly passive income. Only hire a management company that has experience managing the asset class you intend to own.

"The good thing about multifamily is—since the income is naturally much higher—the management company only requires 3.5 to 4 percent for payment."

Kenny Wolfe

Chapter 7

Have Your Cake and Eat It Too

One of the best things about investing in multifamily real estate in particular is you can get a non-recourse loan from Fannie Mae, or Freddie Mac, to purchase the property. A non-recourse loan means the bank you got the loan from can't come after your other assets if you fail to repay the loan. There are five bad boy clauses that could make it a recourse loan, but as long as you don't lie, steal, or cheat, then it remains a non-recourse loan.

If the deal goes bad, then all the bank can do is take back possession of the property. They will try to sell the property to get their money back. If they can't get their money back, then they're out of luck. They have to walk away and absorb the loss themselves.

Non-recourse financing is a major piece in what makes investing in multifamily real estate attractive. It's very difficult to secure non-recourse financing outside of this niche. The commercial properties we purchase are recourse loans, and I have colleagues that invest in hotels that tell me those loans are typically recourse (until you're a larger presence in that space).

For example, if you buy a single family property, you will typically have to do this with a recourse loan. A recourse loan allows the bank to do whatever they have to do to get their money back if you fail to repay the loan. If they can't get their money back by taking possession of the property and selling it, they can come after your other assets, garnish your wages or do whatever they have to do to make up for the loss.

By pursuing and securing non-recourse financing for a multifamily property, you're able to compartmentalize your investments. This means you take on much less risk while maximizing your return. When it comes to investing, that's pretty much the name of the game.

When we buy a multifamily property, most of the time we go with a non-recourse agency loan. Our business plans are specifically based around each individual property's needs—the goal being to improve the net operating income at the property, whether that's from improving the revenue, making the expenses more efficient, or both. Multifamily properties, as well as commercial properties, are valued based on the net operating income they bring in. This means you can typically force the appreciation of your property by using three "levers": revenue, expenses, or both. There are a variety of ways this can be done.

One of the most standard and obvious ways to do this is by upgrading the units. People will pay more money to live in a nicer place. I like to offer something to our residents that they don't expect. I love to give the residents the HGTV feel for what they can afford. Everyone wants a clean, safe, good-looking unit they can live in and be proud of. Now, not all demographics can afford our full grade packages, but we change the level of unit interior upgrades based on the sub-market. No matter the demographics, our aim is to impress our residents.

You can also increase revenue by increasing your "other" income. This can include charging pet rent, creating reserved parking spots, or by adding special features to certain units. Ultimately, the more revenue you can bring in, the higher your property will be valued. There are a lot more ways to create value on a multifamily or commercial property than a single family property.

Another example is that in one of our properties, the leasing office was in a two-bedroom apartment when we bought the property. We converted one area of the space into our office, and we put up a wall (and re-routed some plumbing) to create an efficiency unit. This way we could start charging rent for the new unit. The $850 a month increase in our revenue not only increased our cash flow, but it added

$145k worth of value to the property. $850 x 12 = annual income of $10,200 and divide that by a 7.0% cap rate—you get the value created of $145k. It cost us $7k to add this unit; talk about ROI! Now, we can't always add units like this, but it shows the types of returns we can create by being creative with a property.

I like to look for properties that are missing out on multiple improvements by also looking to see where we can improve on the expenses. I say improve, and not cut, on purpose. You can't gut expenses completely and expect to retain better quality residents. That's why we look to make them more efficient. I've seen owners fill in swimming pools, remove playgrounds, etc. just to save a few dollars on upkeep, but what they're not factoring in is that by taking away amenities, they're going to have quality residents move away from the property.

You have to look at both sides of the net operating income equation. Some of the opportunities that I've seen are where the landlord pays the utilities, but none of the surrounding properties pay the utilities. I've seen the same for properties that provide cable to their residents when their neighbors don't offer that; there is also an option where you can buy the cable in bulk and make a profit each month by billing the residents for cable. The residents get cheaper cable, and you can make money off that cable service. It's a win-win improvement for your residents.

I've also seen where a property that we bought was taking subsidized housing, and none of the surrounding properties were taking subsidized housing. The property we bought was limiting themselves on the rents they could get for those units. Other items include installing more efficient toilets and fixtures. This can lower the expenses on water at the property, and you can pass on some of those savings to your residents. Again, win-win for our residents and our investor group is what we aim to achieve at each property.

No matter how you go about it, the end goal is ultimately to increase the value of your property by increasing the net operating income it generates. Once you've done this, you can go get a secondary or supplemental loan on top of the initial loan you got for the property, based on the amount of equity you've created by forcing the appreciation. There is a new appraisal involved and the lender will typically give you 70-75% of the new valuation less your current loan amount when you close the supplemental or secondary loan.

By doing this, if you have investors you're working with, you can give them back their initial investment in a very short amount of time. We've done this multiple times and the investors love it! Who doesn't like getting the majority of their initial equity out AND retaining a cash flowing asset? The proceeds you give back to your investors are not taxed at that time, so the investors can re-invest that money as they see fit. As long as they can beat the interest rate on that secondary loan on any new investments they use the proceeds on, then they'll come out on top. And another awesome feature of this type of investment move is that the rent you collect is paying down this loan for you. It's akin to an insurance company using float to invest. It's truly a beautiful thing!

And this is what I mean by you can have your cake and eat it too. For example, if you are able pull out $2.5 million of equity on a multifamily property at a five percent interest rate, your residents will already be paying this loan down for you with their rent checks each month. This enables you to give this money out to your investors in a tax shielded manner.

There's no other asset I've seen that allows you to actually retain the asset, get cash flow, pull your money out, and then reinvest it in a tax efficient way. I always tell potential investors that I'm going to get them their money back as fast as I possibly can. That's our first goal when buying an investment property.

My top priority when I purchase a property is to develop a business plan to force appreciation, and then get investors their money back so they can reinvest it with my company or use as they see fit. Once this is done, investors still earn cash flow for as long as we hold the property.

Invest Like a Wolfe

The non-recourse financing available for multifamily real estate is an incredible advantage. It allows you as the landlord to minimize your risk while maximizing your return. This is the name of the game when it comes to any kind of investing. To improve the value of your property once you've purchased it, you have to either increase the income it generates, decrease expenses, or both. Multifamily and commercial real estate properties are valued based on the net operating income they generate. When your property appreciates in value, you can typically get a secondary or supplemental loan based on the equity you've created in order to give investors back their money. This supplemental loan is paid for by your residents, allowing you to retain the property, generate cash flow, and pull money out to reinvest in a tax efficient manner.

"There's no other asset I've seen that allows you to actually retain the asset, get cash flow, pull your money out, and then reinvest it in a tax efficient way."

Kenny Wolfe

Chapter 8

Generating High, Consistent Yields

When developers build new multifamily housing, they almost always build A class properties. This is due to higher land, materials, and labor costs. So there is really no way to create more working-class housing; eventually A class properties turn into B class properties, but that typically takes a long time. I've got a buddy who lives down in Georgetown, Texas, and he works with their city council. He has asked me many times, "How do we create more affordable, working-class housing?"

The truth is it's just not possible. You can't build your way out of a working-class housing shortage. Where I live near Dallas, it costs about $168,000 per unit to build a brand new apartment complex. This requires the owner to charge a substantial amount for rent. There is no good way to make a brand new building more affordable for the average renter. There are subsidized multifamily properties, but those tend to be marketed toward the lower end demographics.

The only way a new apartment can be made more affordable is by making the units themselves smaller, or by building it in a less desirable location. Those two solutions have their downsides for the residents. People don't want to live in a cramped apartment, and they also tend to not want to live way far away from jobs, shopping, etc.

Because of this, mostly what we're seeing is that nobody builds new B and C class apartments because the numbers just don't work. It just doesn't make any sense. The only way to make money with new construction is if you build an A class apartment complex due to the higher cost to build the asset.

This means that existing multifamily rental properties will always maintain a certain value over the long term. In fact, they will be forced to go up in value consistently. As the middle class grows in number, there is less middle class housing available. If they do lose a lot of value, then it tends to be due to the debt side of the transaction because the demand for them is always going to be increasing, while the supply remains mostly static. Again, this is over the long-term; there will be periods in the short-term where owners overpaid and aren't able to weather the few years of stagnant paychecks or poor available financing options.

In multifamily real estate, those who hold the properties longer and continually improve the properties will do better over the long-term than those that are in it for the quick cash.

Transactional costs (broker fees, legal fees, pre-payment penalties, etc.) are all a drag on the investors' returns, and by holding it long-term the investor(s) are taking advantage of the tax shield that comes with owning real estate. The cash flow is also a perk, and to have that coming in steadily is the dream! If you have plenty of monthly cash flow coming in, and your property is run by a competent manager, a multifamily property is one of the easiest assets to maintain and profit from.

Commercial properties are similar as long as you look for NNN or NN leases on commercial properties. There is even less operational risk in commercial compared to multifamily. In commercial real estate, the long-term guaranteed leases are a blessing and a curse. If the market allows you to charge more rent for your commercial property, then during that long-term lease, you aren't able to raise rent. But on the flip side, your leases are guaranteed by strong tenants, so there is less risk in evictions. We like to buy high-credit, publicly traded commercial properties that are guaranteed by the parent company. Steady cash flow is the name of the game.

In the economic crash of 2008, we all saw a lot of folks lose a decade's worth of savings that disappeared in the stock market. All the money they had invested in stocks suddenly disappeared when the market crashed, and it took these people another decade to get that money back. I myself anticipated the crash, and I sold most of the stocks I owned before it happened.

When the market was down, I started buying stocks and preferred stocks like crazy. I really liked the preferred stocks because I was looking at some really great dividends and had some good upside as well. The common stocks didn't have the high dividends, but had more potential for upside gains. I eventually sold most of these stocks to get into real estate around 2010, and I more than doubled my money. I guess, in the end, the lesson I learned about the volatility of the stock market when I was 16 taught me a valuable lesson about how to play the investing game.

The reason I was able to double my money in the stock market is because I understood the financials behind the companies I invested in. In fact, this is why it has been relatively simple for me to go from working as an accountant in the oil and gas industry, to running a real estate investment firm that specializes in generating passive income for investors through multifamily and commercial real estate. The one thing I would suggest to new investors is that they have a basic understanding of accounting. No need for the full-blown CPA designation, but the ability to read and understand financial statements is key to being successful with almost all investments.

The biggest risk you can take when it comes to real estate investing, or any type of investing, is getting caught up in what everybody else is saying. People often look at the market, and they say things like, "This time things are going to be different. This time the market isn't going to crash." This is when people start to make unwise investments. When prices are way up, everyone tries to cash in. But everything that goes up must come down, at least temporarily.

If you decide to keep buying at pique bidding prices because everyone is talking about how great stocks, real estate, or any other investments are performing, then eventually you're going to get hurt. When you hear the general public made aware what a great investment so-and-so is, it may already be too late to hop in. Whoever is stuck holding the bag at the end of a bull market is going to pay handsomely for it. You don't want to end up being that person.

In real estate, this also goes for certain asset types and locations. I like buying in the markets that aren't all that crowded with buyers if at all possible. We've done this with a few of the markets we're in. We were willing to pave the way. Also, it's not always easy to buy multifamily, so adding the other investment options we offer at Wolfe Investments has given us different levers to pull as the markets change.

Unfortunately, a lot of people don't even consider real estate investing when they think about investing for their future. Many people plan to work at one job for 40 years, and save as much as they can to live off of until they die. They hope their savings, and social security, will be enough to keep them going. If this is your strategy, then you're betting against yourself. That's a horrible way to live!

Growing up, my father taught us that stocks, bonds, and having a good paying job were the keys to wealth. Dad did really well for himself with his plan. He didn't invest in the first real estate deal I put together, and I don't blame him. He wanted to see the proof first; it's so foreign of an idea to own investment real estate in our country. After that first deal, he's now invested alongside me; it's a great feeling to send your parents investment distributions!

Most of America is taught to use stocks, bonds, and mutual funds for retirement. They've been made to believe that's the only way to invest and save for retirement. But you just don't get as good of a return with this strategy as you do with real estate. Most of the talking heads out there promoting stocks, bonds, and mutual funds aim to hit 7% annual returns for all of their projections. By just paying our mortgage, we tend to make 4-5% annual returns on our investments. That does NOT include cash flow or appreciation. We typically crush those 7% annual returns all day long.

According to the Economic Policies Institute, the average American family aged 56 to 61 only has $163,577 saved for retirement. This means most Americans have not saved enough to live off of 4 percent yield bonds in their golden years. This is why many older investors need a stable, high yield investment to make up the difference. The only other option is for them to make a lot of money really quickly, and this typically doesn't happen.

For example, let's say you are doing better than the average American family, and you have half a million dollars saved at 4 percent yield, but you really need a million dollars at 4 percent yield to live the lifestyle you want to live in retirement. Well, half a million invested at an 8 percent yield makes up that difference. This is why creating better yields for investors is the name of the game and truly is my passion. That's a big reason why I created Wolfe Investments; there's a big need for higher return investments with minimized risk.

Real estate actually generates much higher yields than 8 percent most of the time as long as you buy it right. The other great thing about real estate is you don't have to look at a day-to-day update to see what percentage yields are at. So it's a great alternative for those that can't stand seeing the wild swings of their stock portfolio on a daily basis. The returns stay relatively consistent because people will always need housing, and a place to go and make purchases (Amazon can't fill all the retail space), and there is limited amount of supply out there!

Invest Like a Wolfe

It's impossible to build your way out of a work-class housing shortage. The cost of building an apartment complex makes it impossible to build one that people of low to moderate income can afford. For this reason, investing in existing real estate is a good decision for you to make because the demand for it is only going to increase, and the supply of it is going to remain very close to the same. Investing in real estate, therefore, generates higher yields than most other investments, and it is more stable than the stock market. The reason it is not common practice for everyone to invest in real estate is because most people, especially the older generation, have not been showed how beneficial it can really be. You don't have to just follow what everyone else is doing. In fact, doing that is one way to ensure your investment strategy is going to fail.

"Real estate actually generates much higher yields than 8 percent most of the time."

Kenny Wolfe

Chapter 9

Stop Focusing on Expenses

A lot of folks only focus on their expenses when they want to create wealth. They do things like cut out the five dollar morning latte, mow their own lawn, etc. They cut out taking vacations with their family. They stop going out to eat at nice restaurants. They cut everything enjoyable out of their life, and they hope that all the sacrifices they are making mean they are one day going to be rich. It's really tough to save your way to wealthy; if you're only saving money, then you're constantly losing the battle against inflation.

Many people have this mentality that they're going to run their whole household as lean as possible, and that's the only thing they focus on. They don't focus on increasing their household income at all. They accept whatever income they are getting from their jobs, and they focus on living below their means.

Now, I'm definitely not saying you should live above your means. What I'm trying to get at is the importance of expanding your means. There are a lot of financial gurus out there who preach that by doing all of the stuff I just mentioned above, you can become a millionaire. (Save $1,200 bucks a year!) Sorry, but this isn't how you do it. I don't know a single millionaire who has gotten to where they are simply by making their coffee at home every morning. It just doesn't work.

A much more enjoyable option is to create more income for you and your family so you can live a better life instead of cutting everything you like out of your life. When you focus on creating more income, you are focusing on adding things to your life, not taking things away. Your life is meant to be lived, not rationed. By focusing on both sides of the household "income statement," you're able to not only live life on your terms, but actually grow your wealth at the same time.

Life is much more happy and full when you're able to go on vacation, and you don't have to worry about putting it all the expenses on a credit card. It's even better when your investments are actually paying for you to go do something you want to be doing. There is nothing sweeter than walking around Disney World, hanging out on the beach, or camping with the family knowing that you made $1,000 that day. Instead of not taking a vacation for fear of losing wages, you actually were paid by your investments to ride It's a Small World three times in a row!

The cool thing about investing in multifamily properties, and real estate in general, is that if you want to increase your revenues, all you have to do is buy another property. If you need more income to do something or buy something, buy another property to pay for what you want. That's how the rich get richer. Before they buy the new toy, house, etc., they figure out how to fund that purchase through some sort of investment. The middle-class buy the toys first, and then worry about how to pay for them. Be smarter than that.

If you want a brand new Tesla to drive around, all you have to do is create a revenue stream of 1,200 bucks a month. If you put $100,000 into a real estate investment where you're making 12 percent in cash flow every month, that right there is enough to pay for your new Tesla.

You can apply this same principle to acquiring the cash flow to purchase anything you want, but most people are too impatient to go this route. They don't think, "What asset can I buy to pay for this new thing I want?" They think the answer to having more money is just to work harder.

But there's only so much work you can do before you're totally burned out, and if all you're doing is working all the time, then you have no time to enjoy the things you're working to buy. Also, W-2 income is the highest taxed form of income you can make. Buying an asset to pay for something you want to have in your life is totally contradictory to how most people are taught money is generated, but it just makes so much sense.

People talk about how wealthy people are always becoming more wealthy. This is the main reason why. If they want to buy something or add something to their life, they don't focus on cutting out expenses. They focus on buying an asset that pays for that new toy, that new house, that new car, or that tropical, all-inclusive vacation package. Be patient for the toys, and focus on building income first. Then go buy the toys; it really is that simple.

When it comes to people who own rental property, the same concept applies. Landlords who focus too much on cutting expenses in hopes of increasing their profits are cutting their legs out from under them. As mentioned in a previous chapter, on our properties we look to make expenses efficient and not too low to where we're draining the property.

In Texas, I've seen a lot of landlords fill in pools on their properties. It breaks my heart to see someone do this. It really does not cost that much to have a pool in the long run. When you fill in a pool, you're maybe saving a $1,000 a month in expenses. But a pool is one thing that renters in Texas, and really most states, always want. It gets very hot here in Texas, but pools are amenities that residents really enjoy. If you don't have a pool, residents are going to go live somewhere else that does. So by focusing on just the savings, really the owner has just lowered the amount of rent they can charge.

One of the properties I bought in the past has a filled in pool, and you can't bring that back economically. The same owner also dry walled over washer and dryer hookups in the units. I guess he wanted to force people into using the laundry room, thinking he would make more money by forcing all the tenants to give him their quarters. What a short-term mindset! Think of the residents quality of life that was lowered, and in turn most likely the owner was missing out on quality residents and higher rental income.

Our maintenance guy discovered the washer and dryer hookups behind the dry wall. We cut them out, and now we're able to charge $50 more a month for rent in those units. This improved the quality of life for the resident, increased the monthly cash flow, and increased the property value.

I love to be able to offer working class folks options they don't normally get, something they don't expect. In my apartments, we do things like offer wood flooring, stainless steel appliances and nice backsplashes in the kitchen. A lot of owners don't feel the same way, so our competition that sees the rents we're able to get still don't follow our model.

One of our properties is $0.30 a foot higher in rent then our two direct competitors, and we stay between 95-100% occupied. Now, why are we able to command higher rent from the same demographic? We know what the residents want and we give it to them. All residents want that HGTV look and want a unit they can be proud of; if we can offer that same look that fits in that demographics budget, then we'll beat our competition all day long. We also pride ourselves on the service side, so that also sets us apart. By having a quick turn around on work orders and focusing on fixing issues with the long-term in mind, we also attract better residents.

I do a lot of secret shopping at nicer apartments. I see what they offer, and then I try to offer those things at a price working-class people can afford. This allows me to ultimately increase revenues. I make sure to take a lot of pictures, and then the team and I sit down and try to replicate that look and feel. Sometimes we have to scale it down, but again, if we can offer a better-looking product over our competition, we'll get the best residents.

If you choose to focus on both sides of the income statement equation when you become a landlord, you're going to beat your competitors. This means you're going to make more money in the long run. I am able to charge more money per foot than most of my competitors, because we focus on making the property the best in the sub-market, for the best price, and make sure we have the best people that address our residents' needs.

We also offer small things to make the experience better for our renters. We work out a deal with a local pizza place, and when people move in, they get a free pizza. When you're moving somewhere new, the last thing you want to worry about is cooking food on move-in day. It's a MUCH appreciated gesture, and again, it's something that most middle class renters don't expect.

There's a word for doing this kind of business and hosting that I learned in Louisiana—it's *lagniappe*. What lagniappe means is an unexpected bonus, an unexpected surprise. We try to provide an unexpected surprise to all of our residents in some form. It helps business overall, and it lets our residents know that we're happy to have them.

I personally believe that real estate is one of the best assets you can buy. To make it really work for you, you have to go above and beyond for your residents. You have to offer exceptional service and amenities to your residents to keep your properties full and cash flow coming in. If all you do is focus on cutting expenses like a typical slumlord, you're not only hurting your renters, you're hurting yourself.

Invest Like a Wolfe

No one has ever become rich by cutting expenses. You become rich by investing in assets that generate more income for you. When it comes to investing in rental property, you need to focus on providing an exceptional experience for your renters. You can't do this if you're too focused on improving your profits by cutting expenses. If you do more for your renters than your competitors, they will choose you over them, even if your prices are a little bit higher.

"There's a word for doing this kind of giving to people that I learned in Louisiana—it's *lagniappe*. What lagniappe means is an unexpected bonus, an unexpected surprise."

Kenny Wolfe

Chapter 10

Finding Investors

(I'm not an attorney. The following is not intended as legal advice. The reader must obtain legal advice of his or her own.) As a deal sponsor, when my company buys a property, we create a new LLC entity, and then we sell shares of that entity to investors. In order to sell shares as a private company, we have to abide by the SEC's rules. One of those rules only allows accredited or sophisticated investors to invest with in these private placement offerings. These rules go back to the Securities Act of 1933; the rules were put in place after the Great Depression. There were some bad actors during the boom days of that period.

A sophisticated investor "must have sufficient knowledge and experience in financial and business matters to make them capable of evaluating the merits and risks of the prospective investment." This is according to the SEC website. So it boils down to, the non-accredited investor has to understand the risks and the potential rewards of the investment.

If someone comes to me, and they haven't done much investing besides buying mutual funds or putting money into a 401k, they typically aren't a good fit for investing with us. When this is the case, I point them towards good educational materials about investing. There are ways to educate yourself to be able to understand investments. Whether that's college courses, investing seminars, or an experience with some sort of non-traditional investment.

Sometimes there are people who come to me who do understand investing, but they haven't done any investing in real estate before. In this case, it's always good for them to become more educated about their options. If I can't in good conscience accept their money, then I still try to help them as much as I can.

If someone comes to me and wants to invest $50,000 into real estate, and that's their whole life savings, I'm not going to take them on as an investor. Even though I believe in our products, I just can't in good conscience say they're sophisticated enough to know what they're doing if that's their investment strategy. I also want to make sure both partners in a relationship are on the same page. On a few occasions, I had one of the spouses on board, but the other I could tell wasn't ready to invest. In those instances, I've declined the investment dollars; it's just not worth it.

An accredited investor is defined more rigidly by the SEC. According to the SEC, an accredited investor is anyone with an "earned income that exceeded $200,000 (or $300,000 together with a spouse) in each of the prior two years, and reasonably expects the same for the current year." People with a "net worth over $1 million, either alone or together with a spouse (excluding the value of the person's primary residence)" also qualify. There are a few others, but they more pertain to trusts and banks.

Using the two sets of SEC criteria I just explained, I determine who is eligible to invest with my company. The investors submit a questionnaire that explains why they are either accredited or sophisticated. If they are sophisticated, there are more questions about why they believe they are sophisticated. Once someone has been judged as a good fit, and they've made an initial investment, they receive a monthly report from me about how things are going with each investment. I like informed investors, and I aim to provide as much information as possible.

I think monthly reporting sure beats quarterly reporting. I have passive investments myself that only give me quarterly reports, and I think that's too much time to wait before you're informed about what's going on. A lot can happen in 90 days! My monthly reports provide information on current operations, occupancy of the properties, employee changes at the properties, financials, the current rehab work we're doing, and what investors can anticipate happening on the horizon with the investment.

Attached to the monthly report, I always give a full financial report including a balance sheet, income statements, cash flows, and the general ledger. This way if investors have any questions, they have all the information right there in front of them every single month. On top of these monthly reports, we have investor meetings where we discuss the progress at the properties. This gives the investors a chance to ask more questions and to have a better understanding of what's going on in their investment.

In my current investor database, I have 500-plus people. To expand our network, I do monthly MeetUps, and I host guest speakers who have been in multifamily real estate for a long time. I also do presentations for professionals who are good candidates for the type of investments my company provides as well. I've taken a laptop and a projector to multiple out of town potential investor groups; it's a good way to meet new investors and get our name out there.

The hardest investment to raise money for was the very first one. I burned through a couple of Blackberries trying to raise money for the first deal I put together. I called everybody I knew, and it was difficult, but I stayed persistent.

To learn how the whole thing worked, I invested passively in two deals myself. Then I carried around copies of the quarterly checks from those investments to show people that these opportunities are real. It was a way for folks I knew to see a tangible check to an investor without being in the deal themselves. When you're starting out, there's a lot of proving yourself to do on not only the investment that you're trying to put together, but on your competency managing a larger investment.

The second deal I put together was much easier. The quarterly checks I sent out to investors on the first deal I ever did was all the proof I needed to show potential investors how beneficial placing their money with me could be. There's no better marketing than sending out checks to investors. The same is true for anyone who is just getting started as a deal sponsor. Once you've actually put one deal together, then investors are much more comfortable working with you.

I've found it's helpful to find investors who are already working in real estate. If you try to pitch investors who aren't real estate based, you have to convince them to trust you personally, and you also have to convince them that real estate is actually worth investing in. That means two hurdles for you to jump instead of one. Now, it can be worth it to go after investors that might be new to real estate, but just know that you'll have to get them to believe in the investment and you as the asset manager.

One of the things that makes this business uniquely challenging is that if you want to be able to accept accredited and sophisticated investors, then you can't publicly solicit for potential investors. I can't go put up a billboard to raise money for a specific investment unless I am only accepting accredited investors. So that means a LOT of in-person meetings, phone calls, and other networking that needs to take place in-between investment offerings.

One of the things I've done to make the service I provide stand out is, I've made my minimum investment requirements lower than what other deal sponsors typically accept. I do this because I want the first time passive investor to feel comfortable working with me, and to be able to introduce these wonderful wealth building machines to those that are just starting out.

If the minimum investment I required was $100,000 or more, which is pretty common, then I wouldn't attract any first timers. The best way to grow your network is by appealing to all accredited or sophisticated investors, because they will benefit greatly and want to share the success they've had with others. Word of mouth marketing is how we get a lot of introductions to potential investors. Building a good relationship with your investors is absolutely critical for success.

Relationships are everything in real estate. As a deal sponsor, you're bringing together a big group of investors, and you're responsible for making them all happy because it's mostly their money you're using to generate returns. You have to put other people ahead of yourself, or you won't last in this business very long.

You have to build good relationships with your lenders as well. Some gurus will tell you that you should diversify your lenders, but I believe you should do the opposite. For example, the second deal I bought, I used the same lender I used for the first deal I ever did. This second deal was in rough shape. It was in a good location, but it really needed to be fixed up. The tenants who lived in it were equally rough around the edges. On our due diligence walk through, we counted 16 mattresses in a three-bedroom apartment! There were a lot of holes in the walls, etc. Lenders will typically lend out more money for the purchase of clean, stable properties.

I had to prove to the lender that I was going to improve the property before they would agree to lend me the money for it. Working with the same lender I worked with for my first deal actually turned out to be a huge advantage. Because the first property they lent me money for had done so well, they were willing to take a little more risk with this second property. In the end, I secured a loan at a good rate that a lender would not typically give to a first time buyer for this type of property.

Because the lender was willing to work with me, we were able to improve the property for the residents who lived there. They thanked us for what we did. Even the police department thanked us for cleaning the place up and improving that area of the community. The single family neighbors thanked us. We made a big community impact with our investment.

All in all, this business is about helping people. To be a successful deal sponsor, this has to be your end goal. You have to want to improve the lives of everyone you work with, from the investors to the residents. This is the best way to attract investors, and the best way to ensure your continued success.

Invest Like a Wolfe

For investors to be able to invest with you, they have to either be an accredited investor, or a sophisticated investor. If they are neither, then it is best to direct them to educational resources about investing, and then have them come back to you once they're educated. When you are pitching your services to potential investors, make sure they have invested in real estate before, or that they are at least comfortable with the idea. You don't want to have to convince them that real estate is a good investment, and that the opportunity you provide is the one they should go for all at once. This can be an uphill battle. Overall, the best marketing you can do in this business is create word of mouth by helping investors achieve their financial goals and improving quality of life for your residents.

"Relationships are everything in real estate."

Kenny Wolfe

Chapter 11

You Have Options Waiting for You

My company offers investors *four different options* they can choose from when they want to invest with us. The first type of investment opportunity we provide is an investment in multifamily property. This type of investment is a great source of passive income and appreciation for investors, but this investment is also highly sought after at the moment.

When it comes to our multifamily investments, we shoot to get 20 percent annual returns for our investors. This is broken up into cash flow, principal pay down, and appreciation. Our goal is to double investors' money within five years, or less. We typically require a minimum $50,000 investment for this option, as I've mentioned already in this book. When these opportunities become available, they don't last very long.

This is why my company has branched out into offering investment options in other forms of real estate, hard money loans, commercial properties, and development projects. This has helped to increase the amount of investment offerings we can put out to investors, and it's helped us be able to have a sliding scale of returns and risk levels.

I used to have investors calling me all the time asking me, "Hey, when's the next apartment deal?" I would have to tell them that I didn't know when the next apartment deal was going to become available. When you have to look at 100 apartments to find one that's worth buying, you're never sure when the next deal is going to come up. Moving into a few different asset classes has made it so I can help investors, no matter where the multifamily market is at.

It's not always a good time to buy existing apartments, develop properties, buy existing commercial properties, or lend money out. This is why my company has branched out into different types of investment offerings.

For our commercial real estate acquisitions, we buy multiple commercial properties, and put them all under one fund so our investors' money is spread out over multiple properties. We focus on acquiring commercial properties that have leases to publicly traded tenants because I can better trust their financials. Commercial property is dependent on location and who is guaranteeing the lease(s). By focusing on commercial properties with publicly traded tenants, their home offices will guarantee the leases.

For example, some of the commercial properties we've acquired or looked at have leases by FedEx, CVS, etc. The parent companies guarantee their leases for 5, 10, or 15 years. So far we've stayed clear of mom and pop owners and franchisees. Maybe we will get to those down the road, but I really like the corporate guarantees on our leases.

At the time of this writing, we're seeing commercial investments earning between 7 to 8 percent cash on cash returns, and another 7 to 8 percent return on principal pay down. This results in roughly a 15 percent annual returns for investors before appreciation. Not bad for something guaranteed by corporate America. That sure beats the market returns that the talking heads push. By acquiring these assets, we're getting a better return at a lower risk than what these same companies offer in preferred stocks on the market.

The lowest risk to reward ratio investment we offer to investors are our hard money lending investments. Hard money loans are when we take on investors to fund loans for other single family and multifamily investors.

We make sure to be in the first-lien position on these loans, which means we are the first to get our money back if something goes wrong with the property. In addition, we also protect our investors by only loaning out 70 percent of the current value of the property, and up to 100% of the rehab money done on draws. This investment produces a fixed, annual return that is paid quarterly to investors, and it's a good option for investors with short-term investing needs, or someone looking for something less risky.

The fourth investment option we offer to investors is real estate development. This is a new category for us, but we've already bought some land across the street from one of our apartment buildings to minimize the risk. Myself and one other investor are the only ones in the project, because I like to be the guinea pig first on new investment offerings. This is going to be a higher risk, higher reward investment. These investments will be more appreciation-heavy from the start, but they will eventually turn into cash-flowing assets.

Because of the success my company has had, we've been able to branch out into all of these different asset classes. Investors have come to trust Wolfe Investments with their hard-earned money, and they know that we're going to give it our all to see their investments through. We've been able to give back and help other people reach the levels of financial success and security we have reached.

It is a joy to be able to offer financial freedom and the ability to live the dream to so many different kinds of people. With these four different investment options that have different risk and reward ratios, my company is able to help everyone meet their investment goals.

I know firsthand the challenges that people face when considering what investment options are right for them. This is why I've tried to structure my business in such a way that I can help as many people as possible.

Although the focus of this book has been on investing in multifamily properties, you can see how beneficial it can be to branch out into other asset classes as well. Once you have an extreme knowledge of one asset class, you can then move on to investing in others to round out your portfolio. The important thing to remember when you're doing this is to never rush into any type of investment you don't fully understand.

Take your time. Grow as you are able, and you can enjoy all the perks of creating passive income with real estate for a lifetime.

Invest Like a Wolfe

Because of my success with multifamily investments, my company has been able to branch out into other asset classes, and offer passive investment opportunities to an even greater number of investors. Creating this level of success has taken years of work, and dedication, to becoming an expert in each asset class. By offering four different investment options, my company is able to help more people reach their financial goals. If this is something you want to do, don't rush things. Take your time. Grow your portfolio as you are able, and you will reap the rewards of doing so over your lifetime.

"Take your time. Grow as you are able, and you can enjoy all the perks of creating passive income with real estate for a lifetime."

Kenny Wolfe

Chapter 12

Your Dollars are Your Workers

There's a book I love called *The Richest Man in Babylon* by George Clason. The whole premise of the book is that your dollars are your workers. They are your tool for creating wealth. They can go to work for you so you don't have to toil and sweat for every penny you earn. *You've heard me stress the importance of this concept over and over throughout this book.*

This is because I believe it is something most people simply don't understand, so it's worth repeating. This idea is not taught in schools. It's not the way people of average income think. There is a lot of fear about money, most likely because it's not well understood. Money has the potential to be an amazing tool for everyone. It seems to me that it's only the wealthy who have a clear understanding of this concept, even though you don't have to necessarily be rolling in cash to make it work for you. Anyone can get started.

I've heard financial gurus like Dave Ramsey talk about getting a second job to pay down your debt. Do you want to spend every second of your waking life working for an average wage just to pay off your debts? Don't you have other things you have to do that you can't do if you work 80 hours a week? On top of all this, even if you do somehow manage to start working 80 hours per week, W-2 income from an employer is the most highly taxed type of income. You're also paying into social security with every additional check you earn. It doesn't take a mathematical wizard to see how that's a losing game.

When you make your dollars work for you, it's a lot more tax efficient. Not to mention it allows you to live your life how you want to live it instead of spending all of your time making someone else rich at a job you don't like. You don't have to sit in a cubicle or toil in the hot sun all day to make money. Your money should make money!

It doesn't matter where you are in the world if your dollars are at work for you. You can be on vacation riding a roller coaster with your kids at Disney, or you can be relaxing on a beautiful, sun-drenched beach in Belize. If your dollars are at work for you, you're making money every single day no matter how you choose to spend your day.

This is why I love investing in real estate. If I'm at my office, I'm making money. If I'm at home watching TV, I'm making money. If I'm out to eat at a new vegan restaurant, I'm making money. When you create a life like this, it's a very powerful thing. The whole world opens up to you.

Creating wealth, and cash flow, this way doesn't just benefit you. It can also help you create generational wealth you can pass down to your family. I help my investors achieve this type of wealth in the most tax efficient way possible. And that's what I love to do!

For example, let's say I'm able to pay an investor of mine $6,000 a year out of cash flow from a property she invested in. One of the great ways I'm able to make use of tax advantages to help investors is they get to deduct a portion of the depreciation on the property they've invested in on their tax return. This depreciation will eat up a big portion of whatever they received in their mailbox. The investor who is given $6,000 from cash flow will probably only end up paying taxes on $600 after depreciation is calculated, instead of paying taxes on the full $6,000. Eventually, that tax shield will catch up to us when we sell the property, but we get to enjoy that tax shield as long as we hold the property.

On paper, the depreciation sometimes makes it look like we've had losses. If an investor takes the money he makes, and then he reinvests what wasn't taxed, it can be compounded quickly. When an investor does this consistently, things snowball, and serious wealth can be generated.

When you invest in real estate, or any investment, your goal should be to grow your net worth. If you don't know your net worth, then you need to figure out what is and whether it's positive or negative. Write it down. It's your report card for how well you're doing financially, and then update that every once in a while to see if you're improving or not.

Every time you invest in and buy new properties, you're increasing your cash flow. You're also improving your balance sheet because you have more residents and tenants who are paying down your loan. You also gain the benefit of more appreciation as well because rents tend to increase over the long term. Even if they just increase a small percentage every year, that can make a huge difference over a five to ten year period.

When it comes to investing, every smart investor needs to have different buckets where they are investing their money. All of your money can't just go into one bucket, or you're taking on way too much risk. Everyone should have safer investments, middle of the road investments and higher risk investments. Anyone that tells you that you shouldn't diversify is most likely selling something. A professor of mine used to say, "Always ask where a persons bread is buttered."

The percentage you put into each of these buckets changes as you get closer to retirement. So it's really a matter of looking at the risk and reward ratios for each category, and deciding how much you are willing to risk given how close you are to retirement age.

If you're about to retire, there's a lot less room for error, so putting your money into higher risk investments could have greater effects on your retirement years. If those higher risk returns don't pan out, then you'll have less time to make up those losses. If you're young, you can put your money into higher risk investments because if they don't pan out, you still have time to recover from whatever losses you may take.

There are cycles in every asset class out there, and the risk reward ratio for those investments can get way out of whack. When more investors pour into the "hot" asset of the moment, this drives up the risk and brings the potential reward down. Markets always correct themselves, but it's usually painful for those that came late and don't have enough cash to weather the storm. Being patient is a key characteristic of truly great investors.

My goal is to always be able to pull different levers and take advantage of different real estate market cycles for the investors who trust me with their money. I work very hard to mark sure I'm always putting their money where it can generate the most consistent, high rate of return with as little risk as possible.

There is always opportunity out there. That's the fantastic thing about putting your dollars to work for you in real estate. You have to be patient. You have to study the markets, and be able to see where they're headed in the future. But if you keep your ear to the ground, invest only in properties that you've fully vetted, and commit yourself to always improving them to the benefit of everyone involved, you will do well in this business.

Invest Like a Wolfe

If there's one thing I hope this book has taught you, it's that your dollars can go to work for you. Investing in real estate is one of the best ways to put your dollars to work for you because it has the potential to generate high returns in a very tax efficient manner. When you take the money you make in real estate, and you reinvest it back into the purchase of more real estate, that's when your wealth begins to snowball. This is how you build generational wealth for you and your family. There are always good investment opportunities out there in the world of real estate. You just have to know where to look.

"My goal is to always be able to pull different levers and take advantage of different real estate market cycles for the investors who trust me with their money."

Kenny Wolfe

Our Mission
Wolfe Investments is a diversified private equity real estate firm focused on bringing valuable investment opportunities to our investors.

Our Vision
Wolfe Investments looks to create value for our investors in real estate to provide a wealth building platform for our investors. We create passive income for our investors, so we can aid in their financial freedom and investment goals. We provide these investments keeping our core values in mind at all times: integrity, transparency, and communication.

- **2010 Founded**
  Invested in first multi-family properties

- **2012 First multi-family property syndicated**
  Lakeside Village in Wylie, TX

- **2014 1st out-of-state property acquired**
  Crestview Apartments in Colorado Springs, CO

- **2017 Re-branded to Wolfe Investments**

  Branched out to 3 different investment offerings

Our Story

Wolfe Investments started out as Wolfe RE - a husband & wife company with a focus on multi-family real estate investments in the Dallas/Fort Worth area. We are now a larger company with office, staff, and nation-wide holdings. From the beginning, we've made our investors a top priority, and we still do. Wolfe Investments continues to grow our company and our investors' net worth by offering an assortment of real estate investment opportunities with a variety of benefits and rewards.

214-227-0779
info@wolfe-re.com

2121 W. Spring Creek Pkwy.
Plano, TX 75023

9 AM - 5 PM
Monday to Friday

Christine Groffie
Executive Assistant | Digital Marketing Manager

Christine discovered her love for marketing while studying fashion at The Art Institute of Colorado. She graduated with a B.A. in Fashion Retail Management in 2009. She manages all of the design, marketing, and event planning for Wolfe Investments, while also keeping the office fabulously organized. When she's not working, Christine can usually be found indulging her love for tacos on a patio somewhere, attending live shows of her favorite Texas Country artists, or baking a fresh batch of gluten free cupcakes.

Coy Christensen
Asset Manager

Coy has over 15 years of residential and commercial construction experience. His vast skill set in everything from framing, electrical, plumbing, to cabinetmaking has given him a deep understanding of each stage of the real estate development process. Before joining the team, Coy worked in management and developed valuable relationships with investors, property managers, and contractors. Outside of work, he spends his time traveling, playing a multitude of instruments (including guitar, bass, and keys), and writing the next great American novel.

Frequently Asked Questions

What is the minimum investment amount?

The minimum investment amount varies for each acquisition, but is typically $25,000 to $50,000 per investment offering.

How often do you make distributions? When will I get a check?

We aim for quarterly distributions - often beginning the first quarter after takeover. These properties are businesses, so the distribution amounts will vary from quarter to quarter. Timing of the first distribution will also vary for each acquisition and will be discussed when a specific asset is on the table.

Will there be any ramifications to my personal taxes?

You will receive a K-1 from the entity you are invested in, with the exception of hard money loans. There are tax benefits to holding real estate, but please talk to your CPA to see how it might impact you.

What are the typical returns for investors?

There are three main types of returns from real estate; cash flow, principal pay-down, and appreciation. These returns will vary from property to property, so, please, contact us for more specific information regarding total returns.

Can I use my IRA to invest?

Yes, you can use your self-directed IRA ,or solo 401(k), to invest in our offerings. Contact your CPA to learn the details.

How can I view your current offerings?

Due to SEC regulations, we are unable to publicly list ,or advertise, our current offerings. Contact us if you're interested in becoming an investor.

INVESTING IN THE DREAM

Case Studies:

Lakeside Village Apartments in Wylie, TX.

76 units built in 1981/1983

Originally purchased for $46k a door; now worth over $75k a door! We implemented a interior unit upgrade program. The upgrades, rise in overall market rents, and better management has grown in-place income of $593k to today's revenue of $851k!

Investors were given back 100% of their initial equity through cash flow and a supplemental loan after 32 months. We still hold the property and hand out quarterly distributions.

CrestView Apartments in Colorado Springs, CO

190 units built in 1975.

Originally purchased for $57k a door; sold 3 years later for over $85k a door. Investors netted an investment gain of over 60% during the 3 year hold period. The gain came from improved management, upgraded unit interiors, and better exterior amenities.

Ponderosa Village Apartments in Columbus, OH

120 units built in 1979/1980

Originally purchased for less than $41k a door. We put on a supplemental loan and through that, and the cash flow, returned 70% of investors' initial equity in less than 3 years. We still own the asset and cash flow quarterly!